# Je ne sçai quoi: or, a collection of letters, odes, &c. Never before published. By a Lady.

## Anne B. Poyntz

ECCO
PRINT EDITIONS

*Je ne sçai quoi: or, a collection of letters, odes, &c. Never before published. By a Lady.*
Poyntz, Anne B.
ESTCID: T027753
Reproduction from British Library
A lady = Anne B. Poyntz. The dedication is printed in red, and dated April 1, 1768. Pp.vii-xv contain a list of subscribers.
London : printed in the year, 1769.
xv,[1],112p. ; 8°

Eighteenth Century
Collections Online
Print Editions

**Gale ECCO Print Editions**

Relive history with *Eighteenth Century Collections Online*, now available in print for the independent historian and collector. This series includes the most significant English-language and foreign-language works printed in Great Britain during the eighteenth century, and is organized in seven different subject areas including literature and language; medicine, science, and technology; and religion and philosophy. The collection also includes thousands of important works from the Americas.

The eighteenth century has been called "The Age of Enlightenment." It was a period of rapid advance in print culture and publishing, in world exploration, and in the rapid growth of science and technology – all of which had a profound impact on the political and cultural landscape. At the end of the century the American Revolution, French Revolution and Industrial Revolution, perhaps three of the most significant events in modern history, set in motion developments that eventually dominated world political, economic, and social life.

In a groundbreaking effort, Gale initiated a revolution of its own: digitization of epic proportions to preserve these invaluable works in the largest online archive of its kind. Contributions from major world libraries constitute over 175,000 original printed works. Scanned images of the actual pages, rather than transcriptions, recreate the works *as they first appeared.*

Now for the first time, these high-quality digital scans of original works are available via print-on-demand, making them readily accessible to libraries, students, independent scholars, and readers of all ages.

For our initial release we have created seven robust collections to form one the world's most comprehensive catalogs of 18$^{th}$ century works.

*Initial Gale ECCO Print Editions collections include:*

### *History and Geography*
Rich in titles on English life and social history, this collection spans the world as it was known to eighteenth-century historians and explorers. Titles include a wealth of travel accounts and diaries, histories of nations from throughout the world, and maps and charts of a world that was still being discovered. Students of the War of American Independence will find fascinating accounts from the British side of conflict.

*Social Science*
Delve into what it was like to live during the eighteenth century by reading the first-hand accounts of everyday people, including city dwellers and farmers, businessmen and bankers, artisans and merchants, artists and their patrons, politicians and their constituents. Original texts make the American, French, and Industrial revolutions vividly contemporary.

*Medicine, Science and Technology*
Medical theory and practice of the 1700s developed rapidly, as is evidenced by the extensive collection, which includes descriptions of diseases, their conditions, and treatments. Books on science and technology, agriculture, military technology, natural philosophy, even cookbooks, are all contained here.

*Literature and Language*
Western literary study flows out of eighteenth-century works by Alexander Pope, Daniel Defoe, Henry Fielding, Frances Burney, Denis Diderot, Johann Gottfried Herder, Johann Wolfgang von Goethe, and others. Experience the birth of the modern novel, or compare the development of language using dictionaries and grammar discourses.

*Religion and Philosophy*
The Age of Enlightenment profoundly enriched religious and philosophical understanding and continues to influence present-day thinking. Works collected here include masterpieces by David Hume, Immanuel Kant, and Jean-Jacques Rousseau, as well as religious sermons and moral debates on the issues of the day, such as the slave trade. The Age of Reason saw conflict between Protestantism and Catholicism transformed into one between faith and logic -- a debate that continues in the twenty-first century.

*Law and Reference*
This collection reveals the history of English common law and Empire law in a vastly changing world of British expansion. Dominating the legal field is the *Commentaries of the Law of England* by Sir William Blackstone, which first appeared in 1765. Reference works such as almanacs and catalogues continue to educate us by revealing the day-to-day workings of society.

*Fine Arts*
The eighteenth-century fascination with Greek and Roman antiquity followed the systematic excavation of the ruins at Pompeii and Herculaneum in southern Italy; and after 1750 a neoclassical style dominated all artistic fields. The titles here trace developments in mostly English-language works on painting, sculpture, architecture, music, theater, and other disciplines. Instructional works on musical instruments, catalogs of art objects, comic operas, and more are also included.

**bibliolife**
old books. new life.

**The BiblioLife Network**

This project was made possible in part by the BiblioLife Network (BLN), a project aimed at addressing some of the huge challenges facing book preservationists around the world. The BLN includes libraries, library networks, archives, subject matter experts, online communities and library service providers. We believe every book ever published should be available as a high-quality print reproduction; printed on-demand anywhere in the world. This insures the ongoing accessibility of the content and helps generate sustainable revenue for the libraries and organizations that work to preserve these important materials.

The following book is in the "public domain" and represents an authentic reproduction of the text as printed by the original publisher. While we have attempted to accurately maintain the integrity of the original work, there are sometimes problems with the original work or the micro-film from which the books were digitized. This can result in minor errors in reproduction. Possible imperfections include missing and blurred pages, poor pictures, markings and other reproduction issues beyond our control. Because this work is culturally important, we have made it available as part of our commitment to protecting, preserving, and promoting the world's literature.

**GUIDE TO FOLD-OUTS MAPS and OVERSIZED IMAGES**

The book you are reading was digitized from microfilm captured over the past thirty to forty years. Years after the creation of the original microfilm, the book was converted to digital files and made available in an online database.

In an online database, page images do not need to conform to the size restrictions found in a printed book. When converting these images back into a printed bound book, the page sizes are standardized in ways that maintain the detail of the original. For large images, such as fold-out maps, the original page image is split into two or more pages

Guidelines used to determine how to split the page image follows:

- Some images are split vertically; large images require vertical and horizontal splits.
- For horizontal splits, the content is split left to right.
- For vertical splits, the content is split from top to bottom.
- For both vertical and horizontal splits, the image is processed from top left to bottom right.

# JE NE SÇAI QUOI:

OR, A

COLLECTION

OF

LETTERS, ODES, &c.

NEVER BEFORE PUBLISHED

BY A LADY.

The learn'd are happy nature to explore;
The fool is happy that he knows no more;
The starving chymist, 'midst his golden views,
Supremely blest,-- the poet in her muse.
                                        POPE.

LONDON.

Printed in the Year 1769.

MVSEVM
BRITAN
NICVM

TO THE

Greateſt and moſt Univerſal

OF

Country, Court, or City

PATRONS,

AS YOU LIKE IT.

I Addreſs my volume to you, in ink of this *particular* colour, becauſe I mean it ſhould be particularly *red*—and I further wiſh it may be looked on as an emblem of thoſe bluſhes I hourly wear, for
the

## DEDICATION.

the crimson guilt of publishing such mere, mere trifles.

Yet are there others of my sex, who ought, perhaps, to wear a more constant blush, for *workings* of theirs, not long since published. But, as Hamlet so aptly observes,

O, Shame, where is thy blush!

As, by the choice of my patron, I desire no one reader to quit his liberty of thinking and judging, in favour of my sex, but to use me as I deserve; so do I desire you in particular, to stand foremost among the critics; not only because I invite you to it, but as you are a kind of relation, who, in general, as I have

## DEDICATION.

have found, are the worst of all friends.

But, as the same prince so justly observes,

> Give every man his deserts, and who shall 'scape whipping?

Now, I would fain not be in the situation of a poor *Etonian*, who, though ever so short of money, is still forced to pay cruelly for his own cruel means of punishment.

Yet will this prove my too sad lot, if your so powerful family does not assist me in the sale---when I shall be in the state of the unhappy lad just above-mentioned, and pay doubly for my punishment, as being also thus at the expence of my purse.

## vi DEDICATION.

In hopes you will, as much as in you lies, prevent my making a rod for my own (and, at the same time, a *fool*'s) back,

I remain,

with all respect,

Your most and very, &c.

THE AUTHORLING.

*Parnassus Valley,*
*April 1, 1768.*

# LIST

OF

# SUBSCRIBERS.

### A.

Capt. Almiger.
Two Misses Armstrong.
Capt. Aubrey, four sets.
Miss Atkins.
Miss Arabella Atkins.
Capt. Akinside, three sets.
Mrs. Aylmer.
Misses Aylmer, six sets.

### B.

Martin Byam, Esq.
Capt. Byron.

------- Barrot, Esq.
------- Barnard, Esq.
Thomas Bigge, Esq.
John Bigge, Esq.
Mr. Bohem.
------- Bidwell, Esq.
Mr. Baildon.
Two Misses Bowes.
Capt. Bowyer.
Capt. Beranger.
Mrs. Beranger.
Miss Beranger.
Mr. Bickerstaff.

C.

Countess H. Calenberg.
Countess Soph. Calenberg.
Mrs. Corbet, six sets.
Miss H. Corbet.
Mr. Cooke.
John Cox, Esq.
Capt. Colville.
Dr. Clavering.
Mrs. Clavering.
Mr Convey.
Capt. Coppinger.

# SUBSCRIBERS.

Major Cranston.
Capt. Cunningham.
Two Misses Cunningham.
Major Camply, six sets.
Mrs. Camply.
Dr. Connell.
Mrs. Carwell.
George Cayley, Esq.

### D.

Mr. Dyer.
Two Mr. D'Simons.
Mr. Day.
Mr. Dowding.
Mrs. Davenant, two sets.
Major D'Oyley.
Mr. Danvers.
Mr. Dalrymple.
Mrs. Davis, three sets.
Miss Dicks.
Mr. Danmer.
Mr. Duran.
Mrs. Davenport.
Miss Derrick.

### E.

Capt. Edwards.

Miss Edwards, twelve sets.
Two Misses Evins.
Mr. Ether, four sets.
Miss East, six sets.
Capt. East.
Mr. Elphenston.
Mrs. Elphenston.
Two Misses Elphenston.

F.

-------- Fitzherbert, Esq.
Capt. Fortescue.
Robert Fettiplace, Esq.
Charles Fettiplace, Esq.
Mr. Fuller.
Mr. Frayser.
Miss Fleming, six sets.
Dr. Forbes.
Major Forbes.
Two Misses Forbes.

G.

Capt. Garstin.
Mr. Garstin.
Mr. Garstin.
Dr. Gisborn.
Miss Guthrie.

Sir R. Goodier.
Mr. Guest.
Three Misses Guest.
Miss Gerrin.
Mr. Gascoyn.
Capt. Gore.
Mr. Green.
Mr. Gammon.
Mr. Gardner.

### H.

Lord Huntington.
Capt. Hastings.
Mr. Hastings.
Mrs. Hull.
Miss Hawkins, six sets.
Mr. Haks.
Mr. Holland.
Capt. Hutchinson.
Miss Hinton, three sets.
Dr. Hues.
Mr. Huet.
Mr. Hicks.
Mr. Hodges.
W. Hollwell, Esq.

## I.

Dr. Jones.
Mrs. Jones.
Miss Jones.
Mr. Ince.
Mr. Itwood.
Miss Inks.
Sir J. Jay.
Sir J. Johnson.

## K.

Mr. King.
Miss Kepple.
Major Kepple.

## L.

Lord Lindore.
Robert Ladbrooke, Esq.
Mrs. Lenne.
Mr. Lewrew.
Miss Lenno.
Mr Latwoyd.
Miss Leroch.
Capt. Lutchwich.
Mr Littler.
L. Ladlowe, Esq.

## M.

------- Munro, Esq.
Miss Mence.
Capt. Morrice.
Two Miss Mitchels.
Col. J. Mason
Dr. Mose.
Mr. Maud.
Mrs. More, six sets.
Mr. Middleton.

## N.

John Norris, Esq.
Miss Norris, three sets.
Mr. Newland.
Mr. Nightingale.

## O.

Miss Obrien.
Mr. Obrien.
Miss Oliver, twelve sets.
Capt. Onslow.
Mrs. Onslow.
Mr. Oliphant.

## P.

Lord Pigot.
George Pitt, Esq.

Capt. Parry.
Mr. Parry.
Mr. Preston.
Miss Pike, four sets.
Mr. Peters.
Miss Peters.
Mrs. Pratt.
Miss Pratt.
Major Pratt.
Capt. Pratviel.

### Q.

Misses Quins.
Mr. Quin.

### R.

Mrs. Readmain.
Mr. Redaw.
Miss Right.
Mr. Renew.
Mr. Rigway.
Miss Renolds.
Mr. Rator.

### S.

J. Sober, Esq.
William Southell, Esq.
Mr. Spidoll.

# SUBSCRIBERS.

Mr. Sharpe.
Miss Strowde.
Mrs. Stapleton.
Miss Saunders.
Two Misses Stones.
Mr. Stuart.
Mr. Struenſee.

### T.

Mr. Thomſon.
Martin Tomkins, Eſq.
Mrs. Taylor.
Mr. Texier.

### V.

Mr. Vitu.

### W.

Paul Wentworth, Eſq.
Miss Wentworth.
Mr. White.
Capt. White.
Miss White.
Mr. Walker.

### Z.

Mr. Zuntz.

# JE NE SÇAI QUOI.

## LETTER I.

*To the Right Hon. Lord B―――.*

MY LORD! *London.*

--- YOU men of gallantry---nay, I will even style you *Love-professors*---who have taken regular degrees in fallacious affections, and, like other degrees, not from merit, but length of time---talk of *love* with as much flippancy of tongue, and equal indifference of behaviour, as a soldier of sixpence a-day does of *honour*---Observe, the latter, when a journeyman taylor or blacksmith, was thought a liar in every thing he said, if he pawned only his paltry word for it; but the same man, now, by means of a few yards of red, not scarlet, cloth, (for that belongs only to *gentlemen*, as they are called,) and a roll of tape sewed fantastically over it, immediately talks of his *honour*, and is to be instantly believed; though his bare word, as I observed before, would not have been taken for one day's poor pay in the whole week. This is being gulled with words---not things---Nor will I ever believe love can be properly called so, till it has followed its object, as you have done by me, through illness, misfortune, and *all beneath the moon*, as the play has it, without asking, or even wishing, the vulgar return of a penny-worth for the penny; waiting her kind return; and, as her person is the only treasure she possesses, accepting it in the words of Mr. Rowe:

'Tis all she *has*, and what she *has* she offers.

But, of all you women-hunters, commend me to the *Lady-killer*, as I call him, who, the moment he finds a female seemingly to incline towards him, leaves her, as he thinks, to die of a *broken heart*, and is surprized, some months after, to see her walking in a solitary corner of Kensington gardens, like myself perhaps, instead of dangling on a branch of some oak-tree, as a companion to the unfortunate Bateman, who, as we are informed by every puppet-shew manager, in his bill of fare of the day, died *really* and *truly* for love. This same performance could never have been so applauded time almost immemorial, had there never been such a *kind* swain and *cruel* nymph; and, I believe, it has taken such firm possession of kitchen and stable hearts, that no history-doubts will ever be able to bring it under condemnation, any more than a certain volume\*, lately published, will render the first impressions of a crook-back'd Richard of no effect.

If I meet you in the old corner of the gallery at the Opera this evening, I will

\* Walpole's, &c.

even quit Lovatini, who is always *new*, even with an old air, much more a virgin one, to finish the subject I have begun; if not, to-morrow, at the chocolate hour, I will endeavour, at least, to overpower, if I cannot convince you---A woman *overpower*, say you, whose business it is to be *undermost!* Yes, my Lord, but I can tell you in private, that we sometimes thrive best when we are uppermost. Yet, in whatever station or position I am placed, believe me, no time, place, or distance, shall obliterate your friendship, for *love*, as it is falsely, though so familiarly called, would remain with me, like the poor Ghost in Hamlet, only

While one with mod'rate haste might count an hundred.

Nay, an hundred to one if it did; but, as honest Jack says, alluding to a paltry debt of another kind, I owe you a million, indeed, I owe you my love.

Abruptly, but sincerely,

Yours, &c.

## LETTER II.

*To the Honourable Mrs.* ————.

MADAM! *Richmond.*

I FEAR you would not so soon have lost sight of your promised land, as your last so truly melancholy letter mentions, but that you thought yourself, as it is said of Cleapatra, so

———— secure of all beholders hearts,
 Neglecting, you could take them

But our sex are now so multiplied (thanks to good teeming mothers partly, but chiefly to us girls never leaving home, while the army, the navy, the universities, and the plantations thin the race of men) that we are unluckily in the situation of mercers shops, which, by being contiguous, give people the choice of leaving one and finding another immediately. Happy the single warehouse in a country town, and the toast of the same place; both, in their turns, may give themselves what airs they will; and then, as the revel-folks have it, *Mine is the only booth in the fair.*

But, in proportion as the foreigners have too much, we possess too little of that pretty palatable ingredient *flattery*, and I fear you never gilded the pill so but he---I say *he*---guessed by its colour it would taste bitter; for marriage now-a-days is wearing out; and a droll acquaintance of mine says, in twenty years, the *proctors* must turn *procurers*, for there will be no more marriages by licences.

Some ceremony, no doubt, for the decency of our sex, and to promote the great end of a banquet, will remain; for even the beggars leap over a stick, and break a loaf together, that they may never want bread---that night at least. But, my dear and honourable friend, take my advice, and stick to the common bait of flattery; it will do, I will affirm, without even looking for another. Though your gudgeon has broke one line, and run away with one hook, yet will he return. You pester him with the word *marriage*, I fear; but young men, who go to plays every evening, (or any where rather than keep at home,) hear strange doctrine at these schools. Iago, I remember, speaking of matrimony, says,

That diet, which, to-day, is sweeter than honey, shall, to-morrow, be bitter as coloquintida."

And what says Sir John Brute? and what does not say Mr. Sullen, and a group of others, who hate us only because they can't get rid of us? Why, even Emma, with all her boasted English bluntness and sincerity, knew how to gild the pill a little, when she says,

For seldom, archers say, thy arrows err.

Though, perhaps, he was a worse marksman than any of the company. Perhaps you have been too inquisitive after, and curious in finding out, some secrets of his. Few men like this---and Brutus is the only person who forgives his wife for being thus forward; yet she comes round him *en maitre*, and rests it as a test of his love---not for the real value of the secret:

Dwell I but in the suburbs of your heart?

Clever woman!---but she was Cato's daughter, and Brutus could do no less than flatter her again, by saying,

Thou art dearer to me, than are the ruddy drops
That visit my sad heart.

Thus, you see, tit for tat--- Senators and their wives think it necessary to flatter a little; but, like mercury, it must be given with infinite discretion, or it is rank poison. Yet, with all this leaf of doctrine in favour of this same virtue, I fear we shall never flatter each other; by which means our faults will be still so conspicuous: and, indeed, it was a line of Pope's which first cured me thinking of it.---'Tis where he says,

## JE NE SÇAI QUOI.

*Praise, undeserv'd, is scandal in disguise.*

I will not say what you so well deserve, but this I know, that you deserve a better letter, which, from the want of it, shall not be longer than while I subscribe myself

Your most obliged,

and devoted servant.

## LETTER III.

*To Col.* ———.

SIR! *Bath.*

I AM not sorry you have suffered a little by the natural calumny of this place, a tribute we must all pay in our several turns. I have felt it less, perhaps, because I deserved it: for minds are never so truly oppressed, as when they suffer innocently, and could, if they had a fair trial, plead *Not guilty, My Lord*. I often wish a court of honour was once erected in this and every city, which, like a court of conscience, should take cognizance of small affairs in the way of reputation; such as a gentle whisper, or so; and end it at once, without further appeal. Persons thus cleared should have a symbol of some kind to prove they had been injured, and think it would be more becoming than half those stars which only the *stupid starers of the multitude* (as Pope calls them) so much admire. Though the attacks, public and private, on your reputation are to me but a test of your transcendent merit. The richest fruits are ever most pecked at by mischievous and hungry birds; and I fear it is often more from hunger than ill-will that the schemes of calumny prevail, as table-hunters must do something to merit the bread they gather there; and so, like Polonius, to please the heir-apparent, swear the cloud is an owl, a camel, or a whale.---I was too far *let down the wind,* (as Othello has it,) to raise any calumnies. *Declin'd into the vale of years,* (Shakespear again), and not *form'd in the prodigality of Nature,* (still spouting, you'll say); for you might have gone *in* and *out* of my apartment, unsuspected. --- But---but---but---fill up that chasm of mine, dear Colonel, with any thing you best approve---a woman can't.

But when I wished and laboured to be the companion of your *softer hours,* why would you quit peace, to engage in such an unequal fight, as must be the case, with all the tabby aunts of your new conquest? The gauntlet of the whole family must be run, and cruelly too, ere you can be (as Iago says) *medicin'd to that sweet sleep which thou hadst yesterday!* All you can plead is the old one of your sex, a dear love of variety;---and tho' you have a rose, yet will you animals, called *Men*, rather make your fingers bleed by gathering one of your own choice, than smell at that which (like myself) I hoped would ever be in your bosom.

Ah! me!---well---and did you *hang over her enamour'd?* Did you call her *the goddess of your idolatry?* that *she was so exquisite a musician, she could sing the savageness out of a bear?* that *she might lie by an Emperor's side, and command him tasks; and so on, world without end, Amen!*---Well! I'll be hanged if I am not jealous.---Yes, my dear Colonel, that jealousy which only can arise from excess of love. *You shall not see me weep,* says poor Lear, yet will it transpire by my servant perhaps, that, like David, *I have watered my couch with my tears*---Poor Eloisa is all my comfort---She finds words to my ideas---With her I can truly say,

I waste the matin lamp in sighs for thee,
Thy image steals between my *work* and me—

I have taken the liberty to change a word there---for one, whose reputation has been singed as mine, is supposed to be so deserted by the Deity, as not to be admitted, should she knock ever so loud---Cruel world!---*Let her that is innocent throw the first stone*---and, well thought of---that last word reminds me of a pretty lady, not far from our mutual acquaintance, who is to be married on *St. Stephen's day*, and says she has her *reasons*---We are all in the dark---but you and I can give a shrewd guess, for that poor martyr was *stoned*, you know---But I forget---you officers only see the outside of a Testament; namely, when you take oaths for a *new* commission.

That yours may never grow *old* is the unfeigned wish of her who glories in being

Your affectionate,

and warmest friend.

## LETTER IV.

*To Sir William ——.*

SIR! *Twit'nam.*

I THINK Dean Swift calls it *leading the life of a spider*, when one is in a state of uncertainty---*a life of suspence* are his very words. I have been in such a situation ever since I had the pleasure to see you last. But, in the moving state I was, perhaps many of your letters missed me.

Th' unlucky have but minutes—

As I passed over Edge-hill, I went to see the fine prospect from the inn, where my dear Mr. Shenstone wrote the following on the wall of some alcove, when in a mood so like my own, that I think no civilities (much more friendships) acceptable, but what we pay for, though at ever so great a price. Every favour, even the poor one of a dish of bad tea from the family teapot, where not a leaf is added on my account, but only the junction of some more warm water, by which means, as the gamblers say, *Twenty may play as well as one*, is some time or other brought round to your ears, and, by the strange multiplication-table of *base* minds, augmented to the old words of *always living upon them.*---Shenstone certainly was in this mood of misanthropy, when he wrote the following:

> Whoe'er has travell'd life's dull round,
>   Whate'er his stages may have been,
> Will own, alas! he always found
>   The *warmest* welcome in an inn.

But a droll friend of ours divided *alas* into *a lass*, and he was a prophet in the affair; for, at this time, is he doing penance for the *warm* reception she so unkindly gave him, though she had never been within the sound of Bow-bell, or heard St. Paul's clock strike the midnight-hour, when the most dangerous of these nymphs are abroad for want of a lodging, and may therefore be styled *Night-errants*. Yet have the worst of these poor creatures been tenderly educated, maternally fostered, and, but for having *ears*, (for their *eyes* seldom are so much their ruin,) might have been now the industrious wife of some honest farmer, and, of course, a joyful mother of children. Yes, Sir William, flattery is their ruin, and you men know the quick or slow poison necessary for such conquests. But I should be equally angry at an expert gunner, designed for much nobler game, wasting his ammunition on a poor house-robin, as a man of learning, wit, family, fortune, glorying in a conquest over a poor *spinner and carder*, the height of whose ambition before was an amber necklace, checked apron, and plain gold ring.

The height of my ambition is to prove myself ever, as in duty bound, according to every petitioner,

Your friend

and servant.

## LETTER V.

*To Lady Arabella ―――,*

*Richmond.*

WELL---sure no woman was ever so disappointed as myself---Though I blame my folly, and feel my loss, yet can I hardly keep from laughing--Why, you must know, a Dutch butter-merchant, just landed, fell in love with me, would have married me immediately, if Fleet parsons had been still in being, when I fatally brought him down to this place, where the prospect has been my overthrow: For, coming from his own flat country, and never having been in England before, he is, all day long, smoking on the hill, and never has mentioned a word of love since. Sometimes he will say so far as this, *O my charming, charming*--- and when I think he means myself, 'tis Lord Harrington's summer-house, perhaps, all the time, or an elbow of old father Thames, under my cottage-window.

You desire an account of our new theatre: It reminds me of what Quin once said to Lord Tyrawley---both wits in their way, and rather rough ones. The former told the latter, that he did not go to see the *ther* players at Bath for the same reason his Lordship did not go to see the city trained-bands exercise.

But while Quin paid my Lord the compliment of his being a great and good officer, he, at the same time, stamps himself the best player; and many would not allow him this, even though he had served so many several apprenticeships to the stage, and Garrick set up for himself before he had finished half his first indentures

This reminds me of that general mistake through life of those who think a number of years, like as in an aloe, brings every thing to perfection, and that less will not do. But commend me to those officers (whose race, I hope, is near extinct) who served during all Queen Anne's wars, and yet perhaps never saw a cannon fired, but staid at some sea-port, to watch the baggage, count the noses of all the recruits, (though that might be difficult too) or do duty at some hospital for sick and wounded; when, during the last war, the blooming sons of Mars (scarce a week from the sunshine of their mistresses smiles) did wonders, and gained more glory in one day, than the old firelocks I speak of would in a century, could they have lived so long---and so, as the Irish say, *Long life to their honours.*

And now, to bring matters to a point, does your Ladyship think, (and no one knows better) that, in love, people must serve such a number of years, first as apprentices, next as journeymen, before they can enter into trade with a fair lady? On the contrary, I think, though still submitting to your better judgment in these matters, that a young active fellow may open shop immediately, nor fear being a bankrupt, unless he over-trades himself, and which, indeed, young beginners are but too apt to do. Well, my Lady, if the men have their jokes about us, we are even with them. Indeed, I think--- I think French gaiety begins to get footing among us, and we women shall sooner get husbands with wit and raillery, than our great grandmothers, with house-keeping, receipts, and methods of making salves; for I should fear, was I a man, having such a wife, left my house should become an hospital for sick and wounded. If we are sick, and wounded with love, our cure is ever at hand; at least, I can cure myself; which is by at once boldly tearing out the blank leaf, and beginning a new one. I should rather keep to the old expression of turning over a new one; and, truly, we may turn them over and over again, before we shall ever read, at least understand them. I may truly say they are unintelligible, or, like the children's Christmas book of pastime, *the Impenetrable Secret*, but the men cannot say so of us---We are made of *penetrable stuff*---an odd expression that, by the bye, if Hamlet did not use it to his honoured mother. That I am penetrated with your Ladyship's good sense is no news---and many of those coxcombs here, who, against nature, quit green meadows and old father Thames, for a candle-sunshine theatre, may think to penetrate me and my designs---they may endeavour it---but believe I am too deep to be got to the bottom of, unless you could transfuse your good sense and good nature into some man, and then I might have hopes of being truly penetrated by him, as is by yourself

Your Ladyship's, &c.

## LETTER VI.

*To the same.*

MADAM! *Twit'nam.*

IN Mr. Pope's sweet letter to Miss Patty Blount on her birth-day, I am a little angry with him for two lines, which, but that he gives us an idea of his love being platonic, would rather be ludicrous, if not indecent.

> If added years to life give nothing new,
> But, like a sieve, let all our pleasures *thro'*—

An expression, I think, rather favouring of a turner who fells, or a cook-maid who makes use of such machines. But would you believe this great man to be a thief, nay, the worst of thieves? for he robs even church-yards. Not far from Gravesend is a common tomb-stone, or rather head-piece, where the thought of these lines is entirely borrowed, in his poem to the memory of an unfortunate lady.

> Here, breathless, lies, without a stone, a name,
> What once had beauty, honour, wit, and fame.
> How lov'd, how honour'd once, avails thee not,
> To whom related, or by whom begot;
> An heap of dust alone remains of thee;
> 'Tis all thou art, and all the proud shall be.

Now, for the divine simplicity of the country bard, who writes, as they love, from pure nature, and which, in both, is the best.

> I once had beauty, and they flatter'd it;
> I once had what they call'd a lively wit;
> Now cold I lie, without a word to say,
> Yet do the neighbours cry, *I had my day*.
> How I was curtsy'd to, it matters not,
> Or by what parents I was first begot,
> I was, but am not, think no more of me,
> 'Tis all the proudest of the town shall be.

Poor girl! she was even with some of those, who, as it may be guessed, were envious of her wit, her beauty, and what not; and I honour her a little for the spirit she shews, and venom she spits, even from her tombstone. Who the lady was, thus recorded by Mr. Pope, never yet transpired; some say it was a relation of the Norfolk family. Be it as it will, she certainly was one of those very few who knew what real love was, and fell a martyr to that noblest of all passions.

I fear the modern race, both of ladies and gentlemen, love themselves too well to love any one else; but, as the Scripture says, *they have their reward.* They may be said to vegetate, not live, and they pass through life, like Dutchmen and women in a foreign country, without knowing, or being known, by any, but their own dear, dear selves. What a life!

The male toilet, like the female one, now engrosses so much time for the outside of an head, that few are in the least solicitous about the inside. I equally endeavour to adorn both for your Ladyship, and am,

Yours, &c.

## LETTER VII.

*To Mr. ———.*

Sir! *London.*

I Remember one of the Spectators is dedicated to *Mr. Methuen*, and I think, as with yourself, that plain distinction of *Mr.* preferable to all the titles of *Your Grace, Right Honourable, Colonel,* or *Captain*, unless such are worn by better subjects than I have found them, and the best of which fall so infinitely short of your good self. It is in true friendship, perhaps, as in true architecture, we must retire to a certain distance, the better to distinguish the real beauties of one or the other; and, indeed, though often so close with you, yet did I never know your intrinsic value, till you quitted England. The mushroom-friends, who have so numerously sprung up in your absence, remind me of that herd which Horatio, in the Fair Penitent, so aptly describes.

One lover to another still succeeds,
Another, and another after that,

Now shall I conclude the whole? by saying too,

And the last fool's as welcome as the former.

But, pray commend me to those, who vainly think to recommend themselves to me, by saying they dined, supped, or walked with you at Brussels, Paris, or elsewhere, and think it sufficient to describe your person, (which any paltry painter or statuary can do) when they would fail in drawing one line of your good heart; and which, indeed, if they could, might give one hopes of their copying the whole, and, by degrees, imitating it.---No, say they, I hate trouble, and had rather walk on in the dirty path I ever have trod, than seek another, even with the chance of its being a much better.

What says Dr. Young?

A life of pleasure is a life of pain.

These *busy idlers*, or *idle boys of business*---I will never call them *men*---have scarce time to sign, much more write, a common letter of recommendation, for a distressed patient, to some hospital, are longer under their *frisseur* than any coquet of the petticoat-order; and (as it was said by old Lord Winchelsea of a certain Duke) they lose the first hour in the morning, and spend all the rest of the day in looking after it. And are these the boasted Lords of the creation?---Well, thank Heaven, besides the Portias and Lucretias of former days, we have modern instances of women, whose actions would throw a blush over the best of these animals; and, as for letters, have not we had, in our country, I mean, without sending over the water, fifty leagues up the continent, to fetch them, a Behn, a Centlivre, and, to the late misfortune of our island, a Fielding? Would to Heaven I had lived in those golden days! by reflection, even some light might have been thrown on your poor friend. Not that I am sorry to have seen a Con. Philips, a Pilkington, and the two Somersetshire authoresses, whose names, at present, my memory does not so far befriend me as to recollect, but you know whom I mean.---Well, by changing names and the sex, the lines to Miss Blount will be very suitable from me to you. I will not be out-done by Pope in sentiment and friendship, however I may in language; but as, in this instance, his very words and thoughts would be truly my own, pray take them.

> May day on day increase, and year on year,
> Without a pain, a trouble, or a fear;
> And, oh! since death must that lov'd frame destroy,
> Die in a sudden extasy of joy,
> Or let thy soul in some soft dream remove,
> And be thy latest gasp a gasp of love.

Now, between friends, he cannot mean a fit of laughing; that would be rather a kind of strangling and painful death---I rather think he would whisper (though not speak loud) those fits of tender or soft *apoplexy*, which we are both but too subject to, and which are not of that nature to end us at once, but linger, linger on, till I fear insensibility must be our lot, if we live long enough. That I am not yet insensible of you, and those favours you bestow so liberally, and in secret too, (which ever should be to a woman) will appear best by enquiring of those, even in my own sex, who, if possible, would lessen every thing of a man, more especially when they suspect he gives his all to one. May I ever be that happy person! to continue which, not only imagine, but rest assured, I am

Your faithful, &c.

## LETTER VIII.

*To Mrs. ————.*

Madam! *Hamstead.*

I Hope not to be the last, as I know myself not the least, in my sincerest congratulations on the state you have so lately and so happily entered, and which might have been my happy lot at your early age, but that------ the curtain of my sufferings must at once drop, or I shall be incapable to be so chearful on this occasion of yours, as my friendship, and indeed gratitude, prompt me.

I am glad you have preferred merit to millions, and privacy to pomp. Believe me, my dear, the words *Grace* or *Lady-ship* seem only a mock on poor mortality, when care and wretchedness have taken hold of us, and a Lord of an husband (I really mean a *peer* in this place, for, otherwise, they are all *lordly* enough) gives sad consolation in a family-quarrel, when every oath is larded with *My Lady!*

I need not give you a hint, of all people, (whose penetration has so often seen its ill consequences in others) how necessary it is to play the politician a little, and not appearing so fond of your husband in public, as you privately may be. Lord Foppington, in a professed fit of raillery, and without a further meaning than, perhaps, to ridicule, has given us a maxim, which our sex ought to write in letters of gold. When his brother, Tom, has been listening very patiently to an history of his Lordship's intrigues, this question naturally occurs: *But pray, My Lord, do you never think of gaining a woman's heart?* To which he smilingly answers: *that, of all things, he hates the very thought of it; for no sooner is a man in possession of a woman's heart, but he never can get rid of the rest of her body.*

Why, *she would hang on him,* (says Hamlet) *as if increase of appetite grew by what it fed on;* and, perhaps, this disgusted his sacred Majesty, her first husband, when, growing cold to her, she sought for another, acted a different part with him, from her experience of the last, and, I am sorry to say it, in order to bring it about sooner, gave him, perhaps, a dose of laudanum.

Rosalind, I think, in Shakespear's comedy of *As you like it*, and from which, you see, I almost christen my idle volume, says,

> Men are May when they woo, but December, when they wed.

The meaning is not incomprehensible, and hope you never will find it out by experience. Lord Halifax's sweet advice to a daughter, and that epistle of Swift's to a Lady just married, will be the surest guides to your present, as well as future, happiness. In some few instances, a wife may play the daughter, and turn the husband into a parent. Men love subjection in a woman, even though we only *make believe*; and that wife will always carry her point best, who trusts to duty more than beauty. The former is *new* every day, the latter grows too familiar, as I fear my letters do, though they bear that very title. As men of sense are ever nearest to folly, in matters of the cabinet with our sex, never, if you would take my advice, refuse, or be cold to, any seeming trifle of this sort. 'Tis often to try us they offer this; and it is in love, as in money-affairs; if people are quick in returning a trifle, more material favours will follow. But the great danger of refusing these *lordly creatures* is the number of dependants in our sex (town and country), who watch every opening to close with their weaknesses; and, by these trifles, get a *material* footing, which their interest will never suffer them to leave, even if length of time did not kindle some little sparks of affection, if we may call it by that name.

As I hope soon to see you, will, till then, postpone the volume I could write on this so feeling an occasion. In the mean time, go back to a favourite song, made public, I hope, for the good of our private selves, and which, I believe, (if our sex are not incorrigible), gained more proselytes to a system of conjugal happiness, than all the words the altar-ceremony enjoin us. Lest it should be out of print, I will trust even to a very treacherous memory, that you may not be disappointed; and so, wishing, though 'tis a short rule of conduct for you, that it may be a lasting one, I remain

Your very affectionate, &c.

I.

To make the man kind, and keep true to the bed,
Whom your choice, or your destiny, brings you to wed,
Take an hint from a friend, whom experience has taught,
And experience, we know, never fails, when 'tis bought.

## II.

The arts which you practis'd at first to ensnare,
(For, in love, little arts, as in battle, are fair)
Whether neatness, or prudence, or wit, were the bait,
Let the hook still be cover'd, and still play the cheat.

## III.

Should he fancy another, upbraid not his flame—
To reproach him is never the way to reclaim:
'Tis more to recover, than conquer, an heart;
For one is all nature, the other all art.

## IV.

Tho' a fairer than you he should happen to see,
Be pleas'd with his choice, and then wish you were she;
Slyly find out your rival's particular charms,
And, at night, be the very same girl in his arms.

## V.

Good sense is to them, what a face is to you;
Flatter that, and, like us, they but think it their due;
Doubt the strength of your judgment, compar'd to
    his own,
And he'll give you perfections, at present unknown.

## VI.

Should you learn that your rival his bounty partakes,
And your merited favour, ungrateful! forsakes;
Still, still debonnair, still engaging and free,
Be deaf, tho' you hear; and be blind, tho' you see.

## LETTER IX.

*To Col.* ─────

SIR! *Chifwick.*

I AM truly sensible of, as I am sorry for, the uncommon pains you must have taken with an obdurate wretch like ─────, to make him even own he has wronged me. This concession is one drop of balsam to an afflicted heart like mine, and who can say, with the ingenious author of the elegy, that

Melancholy marks me for her own.

Yet will I disappoint this vain tyrant. He expects I will write to him, that he may shew a letter spotted with my tears, to raise a further laugh from himself first, and the circle of his idler friends afterwards.────What says Rowe?

———— A dancing, skipping tribe they are;
Fit only for themselves. They herd together;
And when the wanton glass warms their vain hearts,
They talk of beauties which they never saw,
And boast of pleasures which they never knew.

No, my dear friend, I will look on him as of *a jewel long lost*; and, indeed, his ingratitude may be fortunate in the end; for I should have put confidence in others, perhaps been again betrayed, and had the same page of sorrow to read over again.——But, as Wolsey so aptly says,

I know myself now, and I feel within me
A peace above all earthly dignities.

I shall beg you to undertake the (perhaps unwelcome) office of bearing back his picture to him, and the jewels annexed. I had given him possession (as I foolishly thought) of a jewel, according to Othello,

Richer than all his tribe---

But, with him, I say again,

I've done the state some service, and they know it;
No more of that———

Yes, ask him boldly, (for truth is ever such,) if my slender purse was tied so hard, but that the knot would be a *slip* one to him? Nay, more --- but, with poor Eloisa, I must say,

Let tears and burning blushes speak the rest.

Well---your pity is my only balsam---I know I have it in quantity. Poor Oroonoko tells Blandford (a friend like your good self),

———Do, pity me!
Pity's a-kin to love, and ev'ry thought
Of that soft kind sits welcome to my soul.

Could I recollect the words, or rather lines, which Voltaire made use of, when he threw back the King of Prussia's picture, I would spare you the trouble of inventing a proper message. I remember it begins with,

> I received it with pleasure—
> I return it with disdain.

And now, hoping to see you often, (for you are not of that list whom Hamlet gives a licence to quit him, by

> You, as your business and desires shall prompt you.)

I beg you to follow Othello's maxim to a tittle, when that poor man, distracted like myself, though from a different cause, says,

> ———— speak of me as I am;
> Nothing extenuate, nor set down aught in malice;
> Then must you speak of one that lov'd not wisely,
> But too well.————

You know I am with Lady ----------, at Kensington palace, and shall stay the summer: if I can't engage you, let the gardens bring it about; and, by the bye, I can say, with poor Eve, they are

—————My earliest visitation,
And my last at ev'ning———

Adieu, adieu, my good Colonel: and the common saying, that the King may make an officer, but not a soldier, is also equally true, that he may make a nobleman, but not a gentleman. In both instances, you are a proof of it; but hope no proofs are wanting how much I am

Yours, &c.

P. S. A postscript puts me in mind of a friend of ours, who, having tired his company by, at least, an hour, takes leave, as it may seem, and then, pretending to have forgot his cane or gloves, returns, and plagues them again for a whole evening.

A poſtſcript is too often like a mealy apple, or muſty cheſnut, after a good repaſt.---In ſhort, if I go on much longer, I ſhall, as Dean Swift ſays,

> Uſe ſimilies that nothing fit.

But, indeed, when I write to you, I ſeem talking to you. Good writing, Mr. Spencer, the ingenious, tells us, is converſing at a diſtance, as a ſoliloquy is loud thinking.

You ſee, like the good Adam, with his better angel,

> How ſubt'ly to detain thee I contrive.

And I can truly add,

> With thee converſing, I forget all time,
> And while I write to thee, I ſeem in heav'n.

Once more adieu; and, in the words of poor Lucia,

—Know thou wrong'st me, if thou think'st
Ever was love, or ever grief like mine.

Adieu, again.

## LETTER X.

*To Miss* ———.

*Kensington.*

WELL---of all boasters among the modern race of coxcombs, commend me to those who endeavour to pass for men of fortune, when it is well known they have none, by bragging of having been the keepers of such or such fine women, and that their ingratitude in general now cuts off all future commerce of *feeling friendships*, at least with the particular part of them, for ever afterwards; otherwise, that they should have continued to be so for the rest of their good lives, even though it had reduced them to the sad necessity of a last *splendid shilling*.

Believe me, I knew a good girl, who had a head to conceive, and a heart to execute, every thing great and generous in the way of affection; but, unluckily, fixed it on a wretched subaltern, when she had merits, if not charms, to have captivated a commander in chief; but, as the play has it, *Willful will do it.*

Besides the favours she is supposed to have bestowed, and which, had I been a man, would have been esteemed inestimable, she often unadorned her pretty person, I know, the better to adorn his ugly one---nay, I believe, oftener missed a meal than a poor poet, that she might regale him the better at a meeting---thus deceiving herself, the better to deceive him, and make him rather believe she was independent, (at least moderately so) than appear in necessity, lest his then pretended affection should have been taxed by pecuniary rewards, when she too well knew how it would distress him if he was in earnest, and, if not, that she should lose him in the sad experiment. --- She had read Pope too often, not to remember, that

Love, free as air, at sight of human ties,
Spreads his light wings, and, in a moment, flies.

Poor Lady! she is now, as the Scotch call it, *incarcerate* (thanks to her generosity); and this *idle tall boy*, now and then, pretends to send a poor sigh after her, which costs nothing, or he would not be so *mad* (as the world call it), and, with an air of the scoundrel ostentation he so inherits, and which I mean to paint in lively colours, since I am at it, cries, " Poor girl! I loved her, and, as a proof of it, supported her and her whole family, as long as they deserved it; nay, should have settled a pension on her at least, or got the good King or Queen to have appointed her a bedchamber-woman, or some such trifling place or other about court, for I can do it with a wet finger---(observe, my dear, how vulgar he is---you'll know him better by it) --- but---but--- but---" and so leaves off in the middle, like Hudibras's story of the *bear and fiddle*.

And now, to come to the point, this genius (or very pretended genius) has juſt *four ſplendid ſhillings* a day, *kill or not kill*; and as for his eſtate, it is like the poor honeſt Hibernian's, *neither here nor there.*

And ſo this poor girl is to feel a double portion of ſorrow!---His vanity (I may ſay unbounded vanity) is to give her the ſad reputation of being ungrateful, and of having been extravagant---and, with all the gold he can boaſt of, (on the outſide of his coat only) he ſtill declares he would ſend her a cool hundred or two, if ſhe deſerved it; for though ſhe has half ruined him, yet has he ſtill enough to be moderately generous withall. I can truly ſay, with Lucy, in the Beggar's Opera, that

When he comes to the tree, ſhould the hangman refuſe,
Theſe fingers, with pleaſure, ſhould faſten the nooſe.

For I am ſure he muſt be hanged at laſt; and, ſo far from even butchers weeping, as poor Polly alſo ſays, I believe the idleſt of our ſex would not ſhed a real tear for him.

Thus have I endeavoured, though faintly indeed, to picturize a man (if he may merit such a name), and in such indelible colours too, that he may never impose on you, as he has done so fatally on many; and hope, as you know the wretch, by sight at least, that you will say I have painted him in his own proper colours---and would to Heaven I could immortalize him in verse, as Pope does, when he says,

> Whoe'er offends, at some unlucky time,
> Slides into verse, and hitches in a rhime.

Yes, he should hitch so as never to extricate his dear self: and, though a woman, would I contradict this great writer, and, for once, would break a butterfly upon a wheel.

I am, *&c.*

## LETTER XI.

*To the same.*

*Kensington.*

INDEED, my dear, I am not like Juliet, for cutting out my love into *little stars*, to make heaven so fine---on the contrary, I would preserve him entire. 'Tis to you I am obliged for this jewel of the first water, and I will wear him, (so says my dear Prince of Denmark) *in my heart---aye, in my heart's core, in my heart of hearts, as I do thee.*

I beg you will share with me in this joy, by passing the evening here. In the mean time I shall take a short nap, not only on account of our so sudden warm weather, but for the pleasure of verifying what you are left to imagine by the following *idle* ode, wrote at an *idle* hour, and perhaps to as *idle* a friend as ever a fair Lady *idled* with---for a lover should never be a man of business.---Nor can I imagine, while *consols* and *omniums* are almost running over in his brain, that ever he can *consol* my bliss, or give me the *omnium I wish and want.*

## ODE TO SLEEP.

### I.

Come, sweetest pattern of that bliss
    We may enjoy in death!
For constant then will be the kiss,
    When we resign our breath.
No jealousies can then prevail,
    No fears of hearts that change;
The same idea shall prevail,
    Tho' earthly ones may range.

### II.

Oh! think the joy thus to preserve
    Forever what we love!
To hold an heart that ne'er can swerve---
    Such angels find above;

Their bliss, to earthly minds unknown,
    We only can surmize,
But hearts like ours, and such alone,
    May feel, in part, the prize.

### III.

Then, till that pleasing scene appears,
    Of death and endless bliss;
That state of hope, without its fears,
    That never-fading kiss;—
Let Sleep, in part, afford my mind
    Th' imagin'd joy a-while;
And let that hour forever find
    The sunshine of a smile

## LETTER XII.

*To* ———.

MADAM! *Charlton*

I HAVE been, as the Oxford scholars term it, *rusticated* for this three weeks, with this difference only, that theirs is an exile of compulsion, mine of choice.---Indeed, I never knew the meaning of those lines in our favourite Cowley, till at this instant, where, in contradistinction to a town life, he utters these words from some little retreat of his:

Here, nought but winds can hurtful murmurs scatter,
    And nought but echo flatter.

I find no secrecy or sincerity left in life. ---On the contrary, according to Solomon's words,

*All is vanity, and vexation of spirit.*

I never walk an evening but, besides Milton's sweet descriptions, in almost every part of his works, (and which I need not recount to you, who are a living library,) I reflect on that sweet thought of Earl C——————d's, in his letter of advice to Lady F————y Sh————y, then drinking the waters at Cheltenham. When a workman undertakes any thing, how perfect does every part appear?———For, would you believe, a few rules for health, diet, and exercise, which my old aunt Taby would have set down with the formality of a receipt-book, should, in this instance, become the sweet and golden rules of a Pythagoras? Thus, in the morning, he says,

When you rise, full of prayers, from your innocent couch,
Keep all cold from your breast—there's already too much.

This is pretty, as one would say of a bauble we wear---but the evening hint conveys an idea so tender, and so solid withall, that I must repeat it to please myself.

> The dews of the night most carefully shun;
> They are tears of the sky for the loss of the sun.

And now, talking of the sun, do I wish to conclude one letter (as I know it will be a secret in your breast, and that I shall not be exposed on the wheel of criticism for it) in the eastern style; and I will do it.

> May that sun (the eye of our great prophet) which shines in general, with promiscuous rays, on the gardens of the just and unjust, for once reserve his choicest beams for the gardens of my faithful Almira! and when guilt or worldly care open the eye-lids of common minds, may sleep be doubly kind to her who, but too often, wakes for the good of all.

Thus could I gallop, trot, or pace it, till, as Milton says,

>———— the moon,
>Rising in clouded majesty, at length
>Apparent queen unveils her peerless light,
>And o'er the deep her silver mantle throws.

Well---because I can't sleep well myself, I seem flatly determined nobody else shall. Our only watchman and constable of the night (a large dunghill-cock in the yard below) proclaims it to be morning. What says Richard?

>———— The village-cock
>Has thrice done salutation to the morn.

But I am like that part of the inconsiderate world, who, when the world does not go well with them, don't care how it goes with others.

Adieu.

## LETTER XIII.

*To Col. ———.*

Sir!  *Blenheim.*

WE never read any poem, either with that pleasure or attention, as when on the very spot it was first invented, and when the place was also the occasion of it. How often have I wished to have perused Virgil (though in a translation only) on the green banks of old Tiber, and Homer near the trickling stream of a Scamander? But, alas! the fates oppose our unfortunate sex from the cradle---and if we are shewn Richmond, or a Newmarket meeting, our poor travels are accomplished, and we are left to guess where a glass of Florence comes from, a Pericord pye, or a bottle of hock, to welcome at the warm season of the year. Poor Calista in the Fair Penitent, not only speaks of this for the time present, but, according to each fortune-teller's expression, *the past, present, and to come.*

To his, the tyrant husband's reign succeeds.

Every Westminster boy knows the whole, since plays are become so very universal; and I am sure, not an alderman's daughter in a country-corporation is ignorant of the rest, since Punch, and his affectious family, has, kindly (or per force, no matter which) given up the stage to your *Powells* and your *Barrys*; for every stroller now imitates his superior, and I expect to see, in each bill of fare for the day, *King Richard by Mr. Such-a-one, after the manner of Mr. Garrick;* or *Lady Townly, by an humble imitator of the so celebrated Mrs. Yates.* Yet, query, If they will be so humble to own as much?---I rather think her vanity would be such as to take the said eminent actress's name *in vain*, and, though she could not prove herself the same, either in person or parts, yet would

I

she swear herself a cousin, if not so nearly allied as a sister.

But, to return to my colours, which I fled from, (there, my dear Colonel, I am military, in compliment to you, though I hate, at least am afraid of, *standing* armies, however I may relish individuals, like yourself,)---I once read *Windsor Forest* at Binfield, (the very spot where Mr. Pope took the so exact likeness from,) and, believe me, every line improved on me, as would the chamber of beauties at the palace there, had I ever been so happy as to see the originals.

What first occasioned this reflexion was, that here I had the pleasure to *look over* (not *overlook*) Mr. Tickle's divine poem upon *a prospect of peace*, published in Dodsley's Miscellanies.---A thought on solitude (which we both understand, though we may never enjoy) must make a part of this letter, not so much to prove that I know how to cull the best flowers, but through an apprehension that you may not have the book at hand.

But, to the lines---

Sweet Solitude, when life's gay hours are past,
Howe'er we range, in thee we fix at last.
Tost thro' tempestuous seas, our voyage o'er,
Pale, we look back, and bless the friendly shore
Our own strict judges, our past life we scan,
And ask if glory has enlarg'd the span?
If bright the prospect, we the grave defy,
Trust future ages, and contented die.

I would follow his advice, though at a distance, and not aiming at such occasion of retreat as himself---But, since I have the book before me, let me finish with a compliment to your profession, though, perhaps, it only alluded to an army then in being, and not to any future one, unless every officer was like yourself, and every private man like the *honest Trim*, who waits to bring you this.

In circling beams shall god-like Anna glow,
And Churchill's sword hang o'er the prostrate foe;

With comely wounds shall bleeding worthies stand,
Webb's firm platoon, and Lumley's faithful band,
Bold Mordaunt, in Iberian trophies drest,
And Campbell's dragon on his dauntless breast.

After such divine language, I dare say nothing, but that I am,

Yours, &c.

## LETTER XIV.

*To Miss ———.*

BEING in the country, in the reading way, I can truly say I am all Prior one day, Pope another, Swift on a third, and Shakespear every day---What a life!---and yet, soon must I be hurried away to flattery, noise, impertinence, and, all in one word, *London* itself, or its own self, as the dear Hibernians say.---And yet, you will observe, though men are treacherous there to an exquisite perfection in artifice, I must not *find fault with London*, no, not for the world---I scarce ever see a clean cloth there, unless you call a blue one so, rendered such on purpose to cover the latent dirt, hid so artfully underneath, as sluts sweep rooms into corners, under beds, &c. I seldom have a sharp knife, or a fork, not red with brick-dust---seldom a clean glass---and yet, forsooth, I must not, to be sure, *find fault with London*. When I would fain know the sweets of ease there, and *chew the hard crust of felicity*, Pride steps in, swears *I am starving*---that I was caught in the fact of nibbling *the remainder biscuit after a voyage*, (as Shakespear calls it)---For I ever have observed this many-headed monster, the town, consists but of two sorts, of *observers* and *cynics*. If you live well, they wonder how you can afford it; if with oeconomy, and with a view of *giving Cæsar the things which are Cæsar's*, then it is *that we are starving*---and yet, for all this, I must not *find fault with London*. When I would fain secure a lover to myself, some jealous fair (from the multiplicity of our sex there) tears him from me, and away he flies, like a hawk after fresh game. In a village this never happens, and yet, for all this, I must *commend London*, and never *find fault with any part of it*.

Oh! my dear, think only how few of us are gainers by that base city, and then wonder not, if, insensibly, you fall into my way of thinking, and, with our favourite author Johnson, say, in few words,

London! a satire!

Your affectionate, &c.

## LETTER XV.

*To the same.*

IN my last I mentioned that I was *author-mad,* and that I was so attentive to each beauty I find in those I mentioned, as to be almost the very poet I was reading.

To-day I am *Prior-mad.*—— His *Henry and Emma* is my hobby-horse, and from hence comes that expression, that such or such a thing runs in one's head like a *new tune.*

What a master in compliment is he to our sex, in his very drawing up the curtain of this so celebrated poem?

Thou, to whose eyes I bend!

And yet I have heard, and with a degree of affirmation too, that this Chloe of his was only a barber's daughter--What then? Is merit to be totally excluded the cottage, and only to reside in a palace?---Yet such is the world, that, till you and I can be seen sitting under gilded roofs and upon velvet sophas, I fear we still shall be (as our Shakespear has it)

*Touching the base string of humility.*

Well---but now, let us mutually admire this picture of the fallen part of our sex, and which we but too well feel and know.

*Reflect, that lessen'd fame is ne'er regain'd,*
*And virgin-honour once, is always stain'd.*
*Timely advis'd, the coming evil shun,*
*Better not do the deed, than weep it done,*
*No penance can absolve our guilty fame,*
*Nor tears, that wash out sin, can wash out shame.*

The favourite thought in Calista, of her being the talk of

———— ev'ry sober *she*
Who blesses her good stars that *she* is virtuous,

is much finer imagined and expressed in a few lines after my first quotation. You see the consequence of having the book before me, that I torment you; though, if I do this, am I not a *self-tormentor?* being never so truly happy as at present——and now, for the happier lines———

> Let Emma's hapless tale be falsely told,
> By the rash young, or the ill-natur'd old;
> Let ev'ry tongue its various censures chuse,
> Absolve with coldness, or with spite accuse—
> Fair Truth, at length, her radiant beams will raise,
> And Malice, vanquish'd, heightens Virtue's praise

How endless are the beauties of this lovely poem!———I am aware I shall tire you———and yet, like a broker, having no stock of my own, you see I trade on the credit of other people.

I find Otway's description of distress from the lips of Jaffier beyond that of the poem I mention. He talks of---

>  ———— Canst thou too,
> When in a bed of straw we shrink together,
> And the bleak winds shall whistle round our heads---

Prior begins---

> But canst thou, tender maid, canst thou sustain
> Afflictive want, or hunger's pressing pain?
> Those limbs, in lawn, and softest silk, array'd,
> From sun-beams guarded, and of winds afraid---

I think this far from equal to the former author---but, in every other part, sure I am, that Prior outshines all other stars in brightness, no less than magnitude. His description of that kind of beauty which will ever please; namely, the natural charms, which are heightened by the art of dress (I mean rather modest attire) is truly great, and with this I intend, if my pen will permit me, to close this scene of female criticism.

No longer shall the bodice, aptly lac'd
From thy full bosom to thy slender waist,
That air and harmony of shape express,
Fine by degrees, and beautifully less:
Nor shall thy lower garments artful plait,
From thy fair side dependent to thy feet,
Arm their chaste beauties with a modest pride,
And double ev'ry charm they seem to hide.

After this, I can say nothing---but it alludes (or rather the song is taken from this) to some lines at Ranelagh, wrote by the poet-laureat *, and which every body has by heart---I shall therefore only add, I am, with all my heart,

Your affectionate, &c.

* Ye belles and ye flirts, &c.

## LETTER XVI.

*To Lady* ————.

MADAM! *Dorking.*

AS I told you from the very beginning, I am extremely angry with the printer of my proposals for this very book ---inſtead of *by a Lady*, I had wrote *by a Woman*---being at a diſtance from him, he, out of his great regard, forſooth, altered my record, without conſent of the party, and, you know, there may be the ſame difference betwixt *Lady* and *Woman* as what they now make ſuch a noiſe about at Weſtminſter-hall, namely *tenor* and *purport*.

Now, I think, by this policy of mine, I ſhould have eſcaped much critical cenſure, and warded off the darts of many geniuſes, (or ſeeming ones,) who ſit at coffee-houſe windows half the day, and, when not more mischievously inclined, in tyger-tearing a weak woman's character, are sweetly engaged counting the drops of rain, by way of betting themselves into a good dinner; or spelling the last Gazetteer, and wisely mistaking *Norway* for *Normandy*. But, to resume my former hint, by the word *Woman*, I should have happily comprehended all the frailties of a woman, the follies of a woman; and, if any dowager, old aunt, or maiden in her grand climacteric, should say I was too amorous in my writings, my answer would be, in the words of Calista,

Because I lov'd, and was a woman.

Well---that line has opened the wounds of my sorrows afresh.----These men (as we have often agreed in our evening-walks)

While summer's suns roll'd, unperceiv'd, away.

are sad tyrants. They admire an unblmished reputation, yet take great pains to render it otherwise; a slender shape is their hobby-horse, yet are they never at rest till they make it otherwise; a child is the god of their idolatry, and yet, when it is produced, they, like the fine lady who presents them with it, leave it to a distant unfeeling nurse, equally indifferent about correcting its health, temper, or morals, as I, unfortunately, may be about this bantling of mine, this driveling book; careless, too much so, if it is reared or not.----Well---as Hamlet says,

> There is something more than natural in this, if philosophy could find it out.

The late winds have made strange havoc; they have shook all the corn by the ears, and, as old Sternhold and Hopkins has it,

> Came flying all abroad.

I think it was Earl Ch---------d's charming alteration,

Came flying, all a God.

How a single word, happily amended, changes the face of a whole sentence, when introduced by a workman, as I call it, a man of genius, like himself!---Nor will I ever forget or forgive that learned lumber-man, who said of this great personage, that

He was a peer among wits, and a wit among peers.

In his Shakespear, though we are but little obliged to him in general, yet in this we are, where Macbeth used to say,

My way is in the seer,

he, very ingeniously, changed it to *May*; meaning, that even his spring of youth was already in the autumn, or black of the leaf.---Well, how did I once wish to be intimate with authors; yet, having made the experiment, never was any poor ignorant woman so deceived. Commend me to their works only; for, I am told, Pope, and all of them, on a nearer approach, were often less than men.

In the preface to some book, I remember this very thought carried on to its height. "Authors," says that writer, "are the reverse of all other objects; they "magnify by distance, they diminish by "approach. It reminds me of a city on "an hill, and in perspective, where the "spires, the towers, and lofty parts, are "seen with admiration; but, on a near- "er approach, we discover little alleys, "narrow streets, offensive avenues, per- "haps, till, at last, we are taught to "wish our first distance had been pre- "served, and repent, though too late, "we ever had come so near, and, of "course, had our curiosity so fatally sa- "tisfied."

You see what pains I take to keep your Ladyship from making a further acquaintance with me, being now a kind of authorling. If you persist in keeping near me, after the fair warning I have given you, all I can say is, in the words of Hamlet to the players,

The less I deserve, the more merit is in your bounty.

I have the honour, &c.

## LETTER XVII.

*To Miss* ———.

*Greenwich.*

YOU desired me to send you copies (fair ones I fear they never can be) of some lines, in a garden near Dorking in Surry, wrote under a female skull---I am just returned from that gloomy, yet agreeable spot, or, as Cato better stiles it,

That pleasing, dreadful, &c.

The owner (as report says, though common fame is, and ever will be, a common liar) is little entitled to such religious ornaments; and, I am told, it was a friend of his, a clergyman, who gave him all the hints.

But, to the lines---

## JE NE SÇAI QUOI.

Blush not, ye fair, to own me, but be wise,
Nor turn from sad mortality your eyes
Fame says, and fame alone can tell how true,
I once was lovely, and belov'd, like you.

Where are my vot'ries, where my flatt'rers now?
Fled with the subject of each lover's vow.
Adieu the roses red, and lillies white,
Adieu those eyes, which made the darkness light.
No more, alas! that coral lip is seen,
Nor longer breathes the fragrant gale between.

Turn from your mirror, and behold in me,
At once what thousands can't, or dare not, see.
Unvarnish'd, I the real truth impart,
Nor here am plac'd, but to direct the heart.
Survey me well, ye fair ones, and believe
The grave may terrify, but can't deceive.

On beauty's fragil base no more depend;
Here youth and pleasure, age and sorrow end:
Here drops the mask, here shuts the final scene,
Nor differs grave threescore from gay fifteen.

All press alike to that same goal, the tomb,
Where wrinkled Laura smiles at Chloe's bloom.

When coxcombs flatter, and when fools adore,
Learn here the lesson, to be vain no more.
Yet Virtue still, against decay can aim,
And even lend mortality a charm.

I saw a young blooming beauty read them with much agony---I could guess her history, though I took not the liberty to ask it. Indeed, as the Lady in Comus says,

How easy our misfortune is to hit!

One vein and colour of misfortune seems to run through our ill-starred sex; and I believe, from the milk-pail to the diadem, Love is the insidious enemy that undermines all our happiness.

And yet it will never cease---nay, between ourselves, I wish it never may---and I remember to have seen, at a painter's, where Venus is on her knees to

Mars, begging wars and rumours of wars might cease, that love and beauty may take turn about.

However the soft passion might then fail in foreign countries, I know not---but, as to Old England, I do believe more girls in country towns or simpler villages, fell a sacrifice to scarlet than for some years before or since.

All we can say is, that our island not being the seat of war, the trailers of pikes here had little else to do---for the great Rochfaucault says, and with truth, I believe, that

> Love is the daughter of Idleness, but mother of Disquietude.

Well---I suppose you have, ere this, fitted up your temple of death, and wait for the scull-lines to finish it. I think you should have the male ones too---they are in print, but where I cannot immediately answer.

Pray, admit into your cell that instructing piece of Monkish furniture called an *hour-glass*---and---well thought of---I will give you a poetical hit, or hint (whichever you will) relative to time in general, or, as Rosalind, in *As you like it*, so prettily says,

> Who Time gallops withall, trots withall, and who Time stays withall———.

You have Shakespear at hand, (and I might say in head too) so I refer you to the original for all that follows, for now I come to my own self.

# ODE.

### I.

The lover, eager to obtain
    All that his soul defires,
Counts every moment still with pain
    That checks his am'rous fires.
He shakes the glass, he eyes the hand,
    That moves so flowly on,
And swears that time is at a stand,
    As was old Joshua's sun.

### II.

At length he meets his charming lass---
    Few words, they say, are best---
Perhaps the scene was on the grass---
    Need Beauty be undress'd?---
Her time is short---must meet her aunt---
    Then, pr'ythee, let me go---
Two hours are past---nay, see, I want
    One hour to make it so.

# JE NE SÇAI QUOI.

### III.

In love, the minutes are too fast;
   In grief, are still too long---
One we would hasten to the last,
   The other would prolong.
Yet blame not once the minute-hand,
   That ever is the same,
Would you make time for ever stand,
   Be mod'rate in your flame.

I am,

Yours, &c.

M.

## LETTER XVIII.

*To the same.*

NO man bears sorrow better---(says Brutus, when they tell him his lovely and beloved Portia was dead)---I must be, or feign to be, the Brutus now, to avoid that seeming pity of my friends, as it is so commonly, but falsely called, and which, to me, is cousin-german, to bad hearts, to contempt---however, in great minds, it is the nearest of kin to love.

Our friend ------- is dead.---Why do I live to see every one happy before me? What says poor Arpasia, in the so affecting play of Tamerlane?

> O Death! thou pleasing end of all our sorrows,
> Why do my weary eyes still wake in vain,
> In tedious expectation of thy joys?

But, I think, she, at last, sets me the example of what I should do:

Live, Arpasia, and dare to be unhappy.

I think one of the ancient philosophers, speaking of this transition from life to immortality, says,

When the very aged and infirm depart, we had long expected so natural a change---when infants die, it is also a state to be attended to---but when the companions of our sports and pastimes, the equals of our youth, contemporaries of our studies,--- when they depart, it is time to look for the dart ourselves.

*What is death?* says another wise man, ---You see me now---you see me no more. In short, I never fall asleep, but I call it, when I awake, a cruel escape from death. What do we live for?---the next year is but the funeral of a former one----Every day gives us fresh proofs of mankind's treachery and ingratitude---We bury our old friends, and experience teaches us not to make new ones---till, at laſt, we are left on a deſolate iſland, without a kind and friendly ſkiff to ſet us afloat again.

Pope, in one diſtich, gives us a melancholy, but no more melancholy than true, picture of what all wiſe people would wiſh to be:

> Taught, half by reaſon, half by mere decay,
> To welcome death, and calmly paſs away.

Our friend had travelled, not like thoſe wretches of our country, who, as the Poet has it,

> All claſſic learning loſt on claſſic ground---

On the contrary, he was a map of every kingdom he had ſo accurately paſſed over, and he truly fulfilled that expreſſion of St. Paul,

> For he was all things to all men.

In contra-distinction to such unimproved and unimproving travellers, a story goes, of a young gentleman, desiring his father to let him travel, in order to see the world, when he was answered,

> I should be glad you should see the world, but sorry the world should see you.

My friend's valiant exit (for he bore every thing with the fortitude of a Brutus) reminds me of some lines in Dr. Young, with which I shall conclude.

The knell, the shrowd, the mattock, and the grave,
The cee, damp vault, the darkness, and the worm,
These are the bugbears of a winter's eve,
The terrors of the living, not the dead,
Imagination's fool, and Error's wretch---
Man makes a death, which Nature never gave,
Then on the point of his own fancy falls,
And feels a thousand deaths in fearing one.

Well, I fear no death now, but that of the loss of your friendship, which, indeed, would be such to

Your most affectionate, &c.

## LETTER XIX.

*To Lord* ―――.

MY LORD!

QUIN, of ever-facetious memory, being once asked, if ever he *made love?* answered, that he found it best to buy it *ready made*.

Indeed, My Lord, the anxiety which we know real and unfeigned, is scarce repaid by the possession of its best object. For I fear the best of either sex conceal so many realities from each other, and deal so largely in poetical fiction, that, as Sir John Brute says, on another occasion,

These people of fashion have such a refined way of talking, they never understand each other.

Another great cause of anxiety, is that, before marriage, we ever hold the wrong side of the glass, and lessen those imperfections it would be prudent, at least, to see as they are, if not magnify them. We should turn the other end of the telescope. Miss C------, our pretty acquaintance, often took notice, that Sir Harry loved a chearful bottle, but forgot, after marriage, that the same peccadillo would turn out to be sottishness; and our friend, Lord B----- lost all his estate during the honey-moon, who, before, only had the reputation, in Lady Fanny's eyes, of playing the game well.

I have been here some months, and, at intervals, from the work-basket, darning up an old grotto, or making childbed-linen for country bumkin's wives, have been laudably employed in watching village-coquets, and treacherous swains, who, under the mask, one of a baise petticoat, the other of a round frock, have more art than even those bred within the sound of St. James's clock. We boast here too of separate beds often, marriages, divorces, and all these odd circumstances, which you thought were only within the sound of Bow-bell, or rather St. George's, Hanover-square; for, I believe, if conjugal fidelity remains any where, it is among the sober citizens, who still sup on the remains of their dinner, and go to bed exactly at a quarter past ten.

What occasioned me beginning this subject was, an anecdote of love-treachery, (nay, I have two for you) which our village, of scarce twenty houses and cottages altogether, has produced since I came among them. You must know then, my Lord, that the nymphs and swains here make love, as they would buy a pair of gloves, by drawing on one, to see if the other will fit---in other words, never marry, till they try each other's affection so closely, as that the woman proves with child; then it is a serious affair, and they marry in a Sunday or two. For once this has been broke through---and I wish the fellow may escape with his life, for daring to lead a new doctrine---Would you believe the cunning and secrecy of a country-village to be such, as not to give his first flame an *item* of it? till, being at church, she heard another person asked on the bans to the very man who had swelled her waist, and, of course, promised her marriage.

The affair was so serious, that she heard it attentively, went home, and died---The swain (observe, he had been in London once, with a load of hay, and had, in that little interval, learnt something of the courtier at some alehouse near St. James's) thought it would be some amends to blubber, wear a pair of black gloves, (perhaps only though an odd one---for I have known this œconomy played at a country-burial, and a pair serve two, by putting one hand in his pocket), and be chief-mourner at her funeral---but, alas! he was forced to fly for it---the women, *all to a man*, (as Teague would say) armed themselves with sticks and stones, and I believe, no wretch in London, for a certain strange vice, ever could have suffered more, than would this farmer's son, had he ventured to follow his firſt love's corſe, *like Niobe, in tears*---ſo ſays Hamlet.

My other anecdote is almoſt ſimilar, ſo ſhall (as the poſt waits) reſerve it for the tea-table---But I am to tell you, that the lively and giddy-pated Patty is, at length, to be married---You know, my Lord, what kind of girl ſhe is---Little ſaid is ſooneſt amended.

Adieu.

## LETTER XX.

*To the same.*

My Lord!

Before I leave this place, I can't but trouble your Lordship with one more letter, just to give you a picture, if my pencil can, of a pair of characters, who, tired of the chain of marriage, and yet loving each other in the main, have resort to daily stratagems, the better to keep the noose from slipping.

Sir Charles (you know him) was bred a gay Templar, (indeed, I think, leaving out the K, they may be called, very justly and truly, *Night-Templars*) married an autumnal-toast, for the sake (no doubt) of her emoluments, equally as accomplishments, though, I do suppose, he still keeps the former a cabinet-secret from her.

They soon retired to what is falsely, but universally, called a country-life, where the servants are in livery, the rooms bursting with London elegance of furniture, and, in short, though sixty miles from that metropolis, do you never see the figure of a plough, a cart, or, as the commandment has it, an ox, or an ass.

His hobby-horse, when not hunting, is a turnpike meeting, or a quarter-sessions ---is happy to be called from the embraces of his once Dulcinea, to examine a thief, or a highwayman---postpones, after his divine creature is a-bed, and has rung the warning-bell, his visit there for an hour, till she is fast asleep, because the parson, as he went by, left the evening-post, and which he must finish, in order to send it back.

But, to the point of these stratagems I hinted---To inspire fresh love, the very embers of former passion being extinguished, and which, alternately, is practised between them, changing only the necessary modes from one sex to the other;

---he places a ladder, at midnight, to steal (unsight and unseen) into her chamber---she places chairs promiscuously, to break his shins---there is to be loud knockings at the door, as if to apprehend an adulterer with his wife---and, by those difficulties, every meeting affords fresh enjoyment.

She often invents a quarrel---runs away to a tenant's---sleeps there several nights---mediators appear, to heal their seeming differences---and, by being reconciled, she becomes a *new piece*, as you gallants call it.

Articles of separation were once drawn, and almost signed and sealed---the village wept---they laughed---and had an excellent day's sport, and, perhaps, *night's* too.

How shall we settle this point of being new to each other, without these idle finesses? Is there no method?

Eve certainly knew this art, or Milton would never have made Adam call her,

His last best gift, his ever-new delight!

Well---all I know is, that, allowing the frailties of human nature to operate a little, (and Nature will have her course) I think two persons, of same inclinations though, might, *every day, and all day,* as Anthony says of his Cleopatra, be the bride and bridegroom.

These are constitutional foibles, which, if each can find out, may be so softened, as to become no part of a jangle, and might as easily be awayed with, as a pimple on the chin, an eye-cast, or an olive complexion.

However, the idea has made me turn poet this morning, and, as I know it will go no farther, shall repose it with you, as baubles are often left at bankers, lest they should be stolen, and, being worn by others, become, by time, their property; and though, of little value, yet not easily recovered to the right owner.

I am, &c.

# JE NE SÇAI QUOI.

### I.

Tell me that secret, known to few,
How still to man we shall be new,
   When once possession's past?
How shall we make them hope again?
For, without hope, the wedding-chain
   Drops heavy at the last.

### II.

Give them their way, they slight you first;
Oppose them, and, at once, you're curst---
   What shall a woman do?
Be fond, they hate you in a trice---
Be cold, why then (not over-nice)
   They hurry to the stew.

### III.

While yet that fever of the soul
Rages without the least controul,
   The wife still mopes at home;
He revels in some dear-bought charms,
Then snores in matrimonial arms,
   While she, in vain, cries, Come!

IV.

One method only I can find,
The maxim of a female mind,
 To mischief ever prone;
Play tit for tat, but if the fool,
To such revenge, is tame and dull---
 The wife must be undone.

## LETTER XXI.

*To Lord ———.*

My Lord!

It is a maxim of somebody's, perhaps my own, that we generally repent more heartily of our follies than we do of our sins; and I wish I am not too recent a proof of it. I sincerely repent me of the folly, in not quitting London, ere my health, my spirits, and even purse, were in their zenith: for now I shall stand as little a chance of making a conquest at some distant market-town, as a country-squire, of forty years, and upwards, would in London, where his manners would be as odious and irreconcileable to the tempers of the *bon-ton* world, as my London arrogance might be among the swains of a Welch assembly, after the annual horse-race, or triennial music-meeting.

Solitude is certainly pleasing; but then we must have somebody to communicate this secret, of how pleasing this same solitude is----and then, pray, where is your solitude?

No, my Lord, in spite of ourselves, and all we read from books, the life of an hermit is truly shocking. The menagerie of birds and of animals, collected east and west, and canals glittering with gold and silver fish, are mighty pleasant for the first month; but we are born to fly at higher game, and man must be with his equals.

Don't imagine, by this, I exclude woman, as Hamlet does so artfully, in a fit of the spleen, with his

Man delights not me, nor woman neither,

For I am still vain enough to take my sex's part, in part though only, and say, as in the play,

You had been brutes without us.

As we are made to conceive what we cannot express, I have an idea of woman, such as she ought to be; and whether the first created was as perfect, it matters not. A *post-deluvian* of this texture would please me, was I a man, and, I think I know your Lordship so well, as to imagine, the same would make you live through all the days of your life equally well as with an *ante-deluvian* Eve.

A woman, if wise, will hardly ever meddle with worldly affairs. The least mention of these breaks the fine cobweb of love in such a manner, as, perhaps, never to unite again.

The hours of love should not be too many. Separations, even artificial ones, are sometimes necessary, but let them not be too long.

'Tis well the joys of meeting amply pay
The pangs of absence, else who could bear it?

The appetite of love, like that of the body, should neither be overcharged, nor teazed too long by fasting. By the first, a surfeit may ensue; and, by the latter, such a tasteless indifference, that, when the feast is served up, it may be too late.

Why is Love painted blind?---but that, during the sweet state, the eyes see no errors---Take away the hood-wink, and, as Othello says,

————— ————— Trifles,
Light as air, are confirmations strong,
As proofs of holy writ.—————

The mistake our sex make, (and it is but too universal) is, that we think an heart may be recovered as easy as it is gained. "We can all," says Swift, " make nets to catch birds, but not ca-" ges to keep them."

Believe me, my Lord, (and I know it, from, I may say, *fatal experience*,) that it is the test and touchstone of a sincere heart, never, when once it leaves, to be recovered. The quarrels and slights which can be made up with a supper and a bottle, are such only as mercenary minds have among them. Knowing that human nature is so subject to abatement, generous minds allow for this, and, like painters, use a share of brighter colouring, to prepare for a proper fading; so that, even after the ravages of time, the portrait remains distinguishable, if not so finished as at first.

The common tricks of an affected jealousy, to preserve an affection, are only fit to practise on the weakest of all minds. A man will very naturally enquire, if a woman's whole tenor of actions is consistent; and, if not, will naturally say, if there is no love, how can there be any the least degree of jealousy?---for love, after a time at least, is not that transitory fever, which every animal feels, but in a higher degree--- No, my Lord---it is becoming your very self, it is forming an heart to your own, thinking as you think, saying as you say. Nor will I call this flattery in two sensible minds, as I will suppose they did not hurry into the state headlong, without first knowing each others wishes.

Slights, oppositions, coolnesses, and all that train of misery, which, according to Hamlet,

Poor patient merit of th' unworthy takes,

the balsam to this is to be found at home---the world will never give it---the remedy is in one alone.

I have taken some pains, by this short sketch, to prove how happy I should be to be your physician for life. Sure I am, that most of your disorders, real or imaginary, would cease to be so, would you accept the friendship, as you have the bare acquaintance only, of

Yours, &c.

## LETTER XXII.

*To Miss ———.*

WHEN I reflect on the great part of a life already passed, and recollect, from the example of so many gone before me, how little I may have to stay on this stage of being, I cannot but say with Dr. Young, in his tragedy of Busiris, and from the lips of that proud monarch of Egypt,

——— Ah! what is human life!
'Tis like the dial's tardy-moving hand.
Day after day steals from us, unperceiv'd———
The cunning fugitive grows swift by stealth———
Too subtle is the movement to be seen,
Yet soon our hour is up, and we are gone!

And why should not this be a good inscription for a sun-dial? I, indeed, so far from being uneasy at seeing time pass, have a delight in watching the almost imperceptible motion of this kind of life-instructor, and can watch the sands of an hour-glass with more pleasure than the several heats of a horse-race, or the acts of even the best play.---How am I changed of late!---

Talking of plays, I have often thought my life not unlike that vilest of compositions, a tragi-comedy. Two acts seem already finished; and if the latter do not produce more plot, and machinery, and contrivance, *and all that*, as Mr. Bayes says, I care not how soon the curtain drops, and all is at an end.

The farce which follows I will compare to the last scene of life---dotage and driveling---where a pert footman, or more pert chambermaid, cruelly, surely, insults lost capacity, and basely tramples on the last embers of expiring reason.

Well --- happy those unfeeling ones, who live all the days of *their life*, as they call it!--- For I agree with the writer, who says,

The only wretched are the wise.

How angry am I with Dr. Young, who robbed us of the following thought! for I'll swear we both imagined the same, though neither of us could express it so amiably.

> At thirty, man suspects himself a fool;
> Knows it at forty, and reforms his plan;
> At fifty, chides his infamous delay,
> Pushes his prudent purpose to resolve;
> In all the magnanimity of thought,
> Resolves and re-resolves, then dies the same.

If a man does thus, what must a woman do? We know what we can do, and what we can not, though all I can do is vain, compared to what I wish to do for her, whose ever obliged is,

Yours, &c.

# ODES, &c.

## ODE I.

To die----to sleep---No more, we find
This body parting from the mind,
And ev'ry fool would hold the theme,
Could we but *sleep*, nor fear to *dream*.

This bids us smother ev'ry fear,
Till Time makes better days appear---
For Time, physician to the mind,
Leaves, by degrees, each woe behind,
And yields to every wound a cure,
But such as Anna must endure.

When our own hearts are well at ease,
Who can't prescribe for each disease,
And give advice to sick'ning friends,
When health on all their hours attends?

But can the drooping heart receive
Fresh life, because you bid it live!
Words only from *Samarra*'s hand,
Would ill affliction's pow'r withstand---
No---he a real comfort found,
By pouring oil into the wound.

Long as the worst of winters seems,
Chill'd air, fix'd darkness, frozen streams---
Yet spring, you see, revives again,
And turns to joy all former pain.

Thus, tho' ev'n your so virtuous heart
Still bears, like mine, affliction's dart,
Time, which has laid his lenient hand
On woes I once could ill withstand,
May smooth your passage to that day,
Where night shall sudden pass away,
And ev'n reflection shall be vain,
Once to recall a former pain.

This state of mind, I fain would give,
To gain it, hope---and dare to live---
Dare to be wretched, and you'll find,
The best of conquest is a *peace of mind*.

## ODE II.

### I.
Yes, believe me, dear friend, while thus mutual our love,
    It is then, only then, that we live;
For experience convinces, and ever must prove,
    What a pain other pleasures still give.

### II.
See the banquet so costly, so rich, and so gay,
    That can beggar the east and the west,
Is a substance of joy for one poor little day,
    For to-morrow 'tis shadow at best.

### III.
The palace, with all its terrestrial pride,
    Such as Eden itself hardly knew,
Grows insipid at last, and we range far and wide,
    To discover some garden that's new.

### IV.
Costly habits may flatter our senses an hour,
    And the jewel awhile has its charm;
But to-morrow the death of some friend we deplore,
    And the sable must then keep us warm.

### V.

But, in love, my good friend, (such as ours tho', alone,
 And not such as the world may pretend,)
Ev'ry day still affords some dear pleasure unknown,
 That tastes sweetest and best *in the end.*

## ODE III.

Hope! the wretch's comfort, still,
 Feeds my too, too languid breast;
'Tis all the beggar has at will,
 When he loses all the rest.

Take not then my hope away,
 By affording dark despair---
Hope's the riches of each day,
 And its want the worst of care.

To ————.

I ask'd of Damon one kind look---
   Was that too great a boon?
His silence was my just rebuke---
   He lives for *one alone*.

## ODE IV.

### I.

Curse on that lukewarm state of love,
   Unknowing hopes or fears;
Nor vulgar eyes a joy can prove,
   Tho' they may boast of fears.

### II.

Cease, Damon, cease to blame the heart,
   Untaught till this sweet hour---
No proof she seem'd to want in part---
   'Twas but a test of pow'r.

### III.

Compliance on your side has giv'n,
    Unask'd, what some refuse---
Ne'er fear a gen'rous mind, like Heav'n,
    Will once the trust abuse.

### IV.

Come, fear not, but the more repose---
    Unwilling minds are poor;
Name not a doubt---he feels your woes,
    And wounded but to cure.

*FINIS.*

CPSIA information can be obtained
at www.ICGtesting.com
Printed in the USA
BVHW050508040121
596837BV00010B/716